Bikes, Bombs and Baths

Contents

Welcome to *Navigator Max* 2

Primary Framework Teaching Objectives 3

How to use the *Navigator Max* Teaching Guides 4

Air Raid! 6

Please Write Back 12

An Octopus in the Bath 18

Welcome to Navigator Max

Guided Reading
Navigator Max offers accessible texts which will help you unlock the potential of guided reading with children who attain below the expected level for their chronological age in reading. *Navigator Max* is targeted at pupils entering Key Stage 2 at around National Curriculum level 2C.

Thus, *Navigator Max* complements its 'sister' programme, *Navigator*, which caters for the average to higher-achieving groups. Together, the two series provide a bank of fiction, non-fiction, poetry and plays for the majority of your class – with the flexibility to be used alongside your existing guided reading resources.

Navigator Max
Navigator Max comprises short stories, plays and graphic novels. The interest level is matched to the chronological age of the reader, while the reading age is lower. The writing is lively and the layout engaging, providing texts which will motivate and entertain while extending children's reading competence.

Navigator Max texts are designed for use in guided reading lessons and will support children, term by term, gradually introducing more complex language features, in line with the renewed Framework requirements. Used in conjunction with the Teaching Guides, the texts will enable you to deliver the relevant framework objectives, making classroom management easy, while giving children the pleasure of reading complete stories at an appropriate reading level.

A New Generation of Teacher Support
There is one Teaching Guide per term. Each Teaching Guide offers six focused guided reading sessions – two for each story, play or graphic novel – saving hours of valuable preparation time.

Each session is directed at the target group, having a text objective as its main focus, supported by additional word, sentence and text level work as appropriate. The objectives selected focus on the key skills and strategies these pupils need in order to make progress.

The session plans include questions for the teacher and sample responses that children might offer. Each session begins with simple recall and comprehension questions and moves on to more challenging open questions, which encourage discussion of, for example, characterisation, theme and choice of language. Also included are examples of statements which the teacher can add to the discussion. Teachers are advised to select from the possible questions and prompts, in order to target the needs of the children. This will enable children to develop higher order reading skills, essential for SATs preparation.

Quality Stories
Navigator Max fiction contains well-crafted stories by respected children's authors, which will capture children's enthusiasm for reading and writing.

Complete Fiction Genre Coverage
It can be difficult to find texts that are suitable for use in guided reading, particularly for children whose attainment in reading is below average. A great deal of planning time is required to find texts that match genre and objective requirements and which are also the right length and able to offer the appropriate level of challenge.

Navigator Max provides comprehensive coverage of the renewed Framework range requirements and objectives in a format suitable for lower attaining children.

Models for Writing
The short stories will serve as exemplar texts for children's own writing. The Teaching Guides also draw on the essential link between reading and writing.

Navigator Max and Assessment
Valuable information can be accrued during guided reading about children's application of essential reading skills and strategies. The Teaching Guides include questioning prompts to track a child's level of understanding of the teaching objective of the lesson. There are also links to the QCA Assessment Focuses for Reading. This will ensure that you have a clear picture of each child's progress.

Primary Framework Teaching Objectives

This table shows the objectives, taken from the renewed Framework for literacy, covered by the guided reading sessions in this book. You will find abbreviated versions of these objectives on the Teaching Guide pages, and a chart showing the coverage of these objectives for all books in this level in the Programme Handbook.

Bikes, Bombs and Baths – Historical fiction

		Session 1 / 2	Session 3 / 4
Air Raid! by Chris Buckton	Renewed Framework objectives	**Focus on Setting** **Y4 Strand 6: 1** Use knowledge of phonics, morphology and etymology to spell new and unfamiliar words **Y4 Strand 7: 5** Explain how writers use figurative and expressive language to create images and atmosphere	**Focus on Narrative Order: Climax** **Y4 Strand 1: 1** Offer reasons and evidence for their views, considering alternative opinions **Y4 Strand 7: 1** Identify and summarise evidence from a text to support a hypothesis **Writing** **Y4 Strand 9: 1** Develop and refine ideas in writing using planning and problem-solving strategies
Please Write Back by Chris Buckton	Renewed Framework objectives	**Focus on Characters** **Y4 Strand 1: 1** Offer reasons and evidence for their views, considering alternative opinions **Y4 Strand 7: 2** Deduce characters' reasons for behaviour from their actions and explain how ideas are developed in non-fiction texts	**Focus on Setting** **Y4 Strand 7: 4** Use knowledge of word structures and origins to develop their understanding of word meanings **Y4 Strand 7: 5** Explain how writers use figurative and expressive language to create images and atmosphere **Writing** **Y4 Strand 9: 2** Use settings and characterisation to engage readers' interest
An Octopus in the Bath by Ann Jungman	Renewed Framework objectives	**Focus on the Difference Between Playscripts and Stories** **Y4 Strand 1: 1** Offer reasons and evidence for their views, considering alternative opinions **Y4 Strand 6: 1** Use knowledge of phonics, morphology and etymology to spell new and unfamiliar words	**Focus on Mapping the Build-up of a Scene** **Y4 Strand 1: 3** Tell stories effectively and convey detailed information coherently for listeners **Y4 Strand 7: 2** Deduce characters' reasons for behaviour from their actions and explain how ideas are developed in non-fiction texts **Writing** **Y4 Strand 9: 2** Use settings and characterisation to engage readers' interest

How to use the Navigator Max Teaching Guides

There are two guided reading sessions for each story. Shorter Brown-level texts can be read to the end in the first session, then reread in the second session with a different focus. The reading of longer texts may be split between the two sessions. Each session is structured as follows.

Text introduction
This section prepares the children for independent reading by introducing subject matter and text type, and usually includes discussion, prediction and whole-group reading and/or analysis of a short section of text. The teacher should share the session objectives and success criteria with the children.

Teaching strategies
Suggestions are made for demonstrating and practising a particular reading strategy in relation to a specific phrase from the text. Children should apply it during independent reading.

Year 3 is a transition year: some pupils may not have completed all of their phonic work. Children reading the Brown-level books may be at this stage. In line with recommendations for the simple view of reading, *Navigator Max* uses phonics as the main reading strategy for this level. As children progress, they can use a range of strategies to help them when they are unsure what a word says, including the following:

Phonic knowledge: sound out the phonemes in words and blend them together.
- **Prompt:** does the word on the page *sound* like the word you said?

Graphic knowledge: look carefully at the letters / letter strings and the shape of the whole word.
- **Prompt:** does the word on the page *look* like the word you said? Do you recognise it?

Grammatical knowledge: think about what kind of word would fit in that part of the sentence.
- **Prompt:** does the word fit in?

Knowledge of context: think about what would make sense in the sentence and the story.
- **Prompt:** does the word make sense?

In addition, children should be prompted to:
- Attempt unknown words while thinking what word would fit and make sense.
- Continually check that what they are reading makes sense, by rereading and reading on, and then self-correcting errors.

Read and discuss
The teacher listens as children read part of the text independently. It is important to prompt and praise each child, while monitoring their reading fluency and comprehension. Observation gives important pointers to the progress of individual children. They then come back together for a group discussion before finishing the text. This ensures that children are reading the text independently with comprehension.

In order to allow all children to read the text at their own pace, record one of the 'Read and discuss' questions on the board. Those who finish early can think about the question on their own or with another member of the group while the others finish.

Focus on
Children are encouraged to read deeply into the text, using specific reading strategies to investigate one or two pages of the text, focusing on a key objective (usually text level).

Respond and return
The children reflect on the text as a whole, consolidating strategies and teaching objectives.

Follow-up
Two photocopy masters (PCMs) are provided for each story. The first focuses on the reading objective, the second on writing. These activities can be done:
- as independent tasks
- with the support of a Teaching Assistant
- as homework tasks.

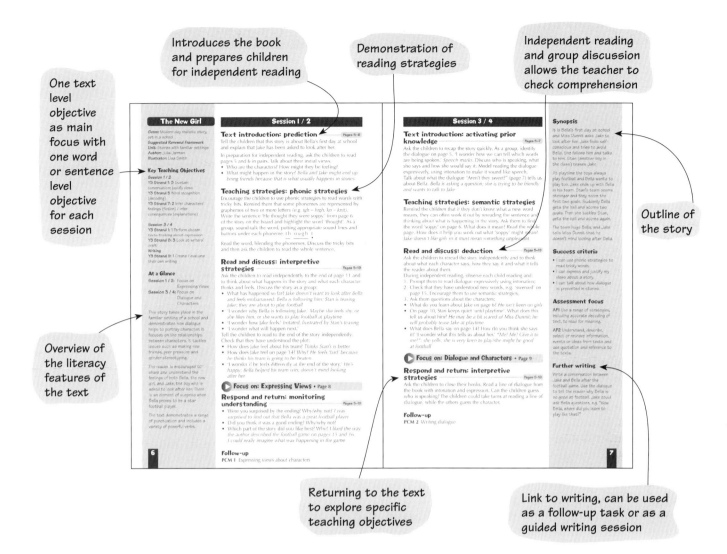

- Introduces the book and prepares children for independent reading
- Demonstration of reading strategies
- Independent reading and group discussion allows the teacher to check comprehension
- One text level objective as main focus with one word or sentence level objective for each session
- Overview of the literacy features of the text
- Outline of the story
- Returning to the text to explore specific teaching objectives
- Link to writing, can be used as a follow-up task or as a guided writing session

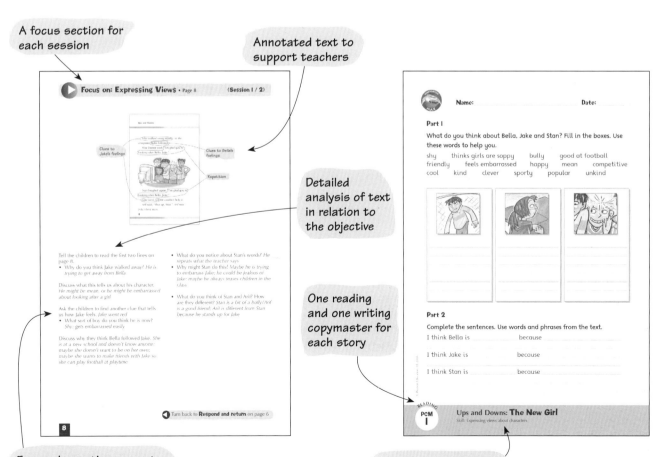

- A focus section for each session
- Annotated text to support teachers
- Detailed analysis of text in relation to the objective
- One reading and one writing copymaster for each story
- Focused question prompts, from which the teacher selects to meet group needs
- Clearly stated objective

Air Raid!

Genre: Wartime fiction
Suggested Renewed Framework Unit: Stories with historical settings
Author: Chris Buckton
Illustrator: Serina Curmi

Key Teaching Objectives

Session 1 / 2
Y4 Strand 6: 1 Use phonological / morphological / etymological knowledge to spell new words
Y4 Strand 7: 5 Explain how writers create images / atmosphere

Session 3 / 4
Y4 Strand 1: 1 Justify views; consider alternative opinions
Y4 Strand 7: 1 Identify / summarise evidence to support hypotheses
Writing
Y4 Strand 9: 1 Refine ideas in writing through planning / problem-solving

At a Glance

Session 1 / 2: Focus on Setting
Session 3 / 4: Focus on Narrative Order: Climax

This story is a 1st person narrative and recounts a childhood experience during World War II. The narrator remembers how he felt jealous when his friend was lent a new bike.

The author successfully builds a wartime atmosphere through small details of setting and action. Suspense is built up through the description of an air raid and the search for a friend. The author delays the resolution by using questions, short sentences and descriptions of emotions. We are left wondering whether his friend is alive or dead.

The story is ideal for studying narrative order, and for identifying and analysing the climax of a story.

Session 1 / 2

Text introduction: activating prior knowledge
Pages 5–6

If necessary, explain the historical context: during World War II in the 1940s, cities were bombed and families had to take shelter during the air raids. Rationing meant that nobody had money to buy new things. Read the opening three sentences together and answer these questions:
- Who is telling the story? *An eight-year-old boy*
- When do you think he is telling the story? *After the war*
- Think about the title and look at the illustrations. What do you think this story is about and why?

Introduce the words: '6d' (pence) and 'air raid'.

Teaching strategies: phonic strategies

Write the word 'dynamo' on the board. Ask the children to decode it by splitting it into syllables (dy/na/mo), sound-talking and blending the phonemes in each syllable and then blending the syllables. Remind the children that some graphemes have more than one sound and to try alternatives. Point out that 'y' in 'dynamo' sounds /i/ not /e/.
Repeat with the words 'cable brakes', highlighting the tricky bits – 'le' (/l/); adjacent consonants 'br'; split digraph 'a(k)e'. Talk about the meaning of the words 'dynamo' and 'cable brakes'.

Read and discuss: questioning
Pages 6–14

Ask the children to read independently to the end of page 11 and to think about what it was like being a young boy during the war. Discuss the story as a group:
- Why don't the boy and Barry have bikes? *Haven't got the money*
- Why are they saving their pocket money? *To buy a second-hand bike*
- Do you think they will be able to buy a bike? Why/why not? *No; they don't get enough pocket money*
- How does the boy feel when he first sees Barry's bike? *Excited*

Tell the children to read independently to the end of page 14. Check that they have understood the plot:
- How does the boy feel when Barry rides off on his bike? How do you know? *Envious – wants the bike to be damaged*
- What happens that night? What is it like? *Air raid; very scary*
- Where do the boy's family shelter? Are they safe? *Under the stairs; boy's mum thinks they are safe*
- Where do Barry's family usually go? *The shelter*

 **Focus on: Setting** • Pages 13–14

Respond and return: constructing images
Pages 6–14

Discuss the story so far:
- 'I wonder what the street would look like after the air raids.'
- Does the boy really hate Barry and want him to get hurt? Why?
- 'I wonder what might happen next.'

Follow-up
PCM 1 Describing settings

Session 3 / 4

Text introduction: text-structure analysis
Pages 6–14

Recap what has happened in the story so far:
- How did the story begin? Explain that this is the introduction.
- What happened next in the story?

Encourage the children to summarise the main idea in one short sentence, and record the events on a storyboard: introduction (the gang all had bikes. Narrator and Barry were saving up for a bike) → build-up (Barry's cousin lent Barry a bike. Narrator was very angry and jealous) → build-up (there was an air raid. Narrator sheltered at home with his family).

Teaching strategies

Look at page 16. Ask the children to decide whether the story is told in the past, present or future tense. How do they know? *Past tense; the narrator is telling a story that happened in the past; the verbs are in the past tense*

Explain to the children that when a story is told in the past tense, the verbs often end with 'ed', e.g. 'It was smashed-up'. Ask the children to search page 16 for verbs with the 'ed' suffix.

Read and discuss: deduction
Pages 15–19

Tell the children to read the rest of the story independently and to think about the other main events that take place:
- What is the most exciting part of the story? *When the narrator thinks Barry is dead*
- How does the story end? *Happily – conflict is resolved*

Check that the children have understood the plot:
- Why does the narrator start searching for Barry? *Because he finds Barry's smashed-up bike outside the shop*
- The narrator felt very angry and jealous towards Barry when he got a bike. Do his feelings change, and why? *Yes, he feels bad that he had thought mean things about Barry; he is scared and worried that Barry is hurt or even dead*
- How does the boy feel when he hears Barry's voice? *Happy, relieved, thankful that Barry isn't hurt*

▶ **Focus on: Narrative Order: Climax** • Pages 16–17

Respond and return: text-structure analysis
Pages 16–19

Add the climax to the storyboard. *The narrator thinks that Barry must be dead and searches through the bricks of the ruined shop for him*

Discuss the ending of the story:
- How does the story end? *Barry is fine; the boys are friends*
- How does this ending make you feel and why?
- Why doesn't the boy tell Barry that he had wished he would get smashed-up?

Explain that the ending of the story can also be called the 'resolution'. Add the ending to the storyboard.

Follow-up
PCM 2 Story planning

Synopsis

The narrator remembers when he was eight years old. All the boys in his gang had second-hand bikes, except for him and his friend, Barry. They saved all their pocket money in the hope of buying a bike to share.

Then Barry arrived at his house riding a bike. The narrator was angry and jealous. He felt he wouldn't care if Barry and the bike were smashed-up.

That night there was a terrible air raid. The next day the narrator went out to see the damage and found Barry's bike all smashed-up. At first he was pleased. Then he panicked and began searching for Barry. He was relieved to hear Barry's voice and they were happily reunited.

Success criteria
- I can use appropriate strategies to read new words.
- I can talk about how characters reveal setting through what they say, see and hear.
- I can plot and discuss the narrative order of a story.

Assessment focus

AF3 Deduce, infer or interpret information, events or ideas from texts.

AF4 Identify and comment on the structure and organisation of texts, including grammatical and presentational features at text level.

Further writing

Write about what could happen after the end of the story:
- Did the boys save up and get a bike?
- What did the bike look like?
- What did they do with their new bike?

Focus on: Setting • Pages 13–14 (Session 1 / 2)

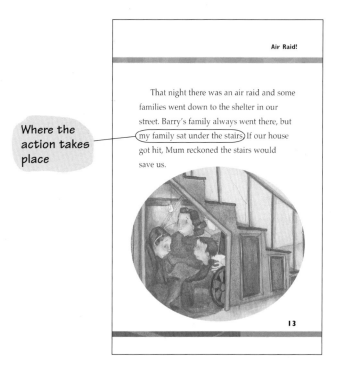

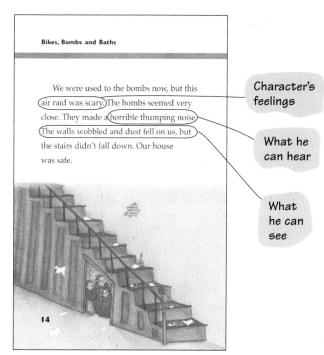

Explain that a powerful way to write about the setting in a story is to describe:
- Where the action takes place
- How the character feels
- What the character can see
- What the character can hear

As a group, identify where the action takes place. Tell the children to work in pairs and to search for examples of feelings, what could be heard or what could be seen.
Prompts:
- How is the boy feeling?
- What does he hear?
- What does he see?

Record these examples in a grid:

Where the action takes place	How the character feels	What the character can see	What the character can hear
Family sit under stairs	This air raid was scary	Walls wobbled Dust fell on us	Horrible thumping noise

Ask the children to carry out a similar exercise on page 15. No sounds are mentioned, but they could suggest what might be heard.

Turn back to **Respond and return** on page 6

Focus on: Narrative Order: Climax (Session 3 / 4)
• Pages 16–17

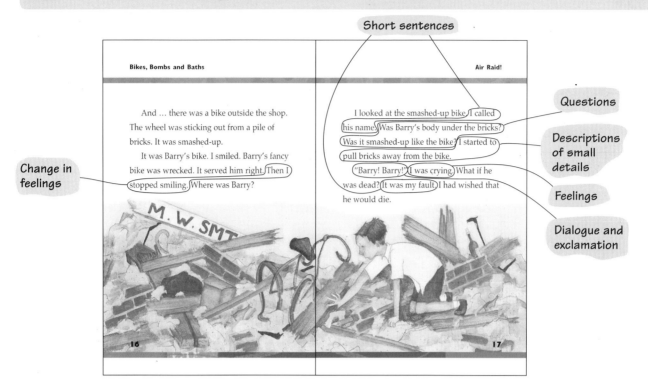

Ask the children to read these pages again. How do they feel when they read this? Explain that the author has written this part of the story in a special way to make you feel very involved in the search and worried about Barry. Tell them that this is the climax of the story, when the action reaches the most exciting part. Sometimes we don't know what will happen next and we are on the edge of our seats.

Analysis
Ask the children questions that will help them to analyse the climax:
- Can you find an example of a sentence that tells us the narrator is suddenly worried about Barry? *'Then I stopped smiling.'*
- Why do you think the author used short sentences? *They create suspense; they sound urgent.* Read them in a frantic manner to demonstrate how they add impact.

Tell the children to read any questions aloud with expression, as if they are the boy searching for Barry.
- Why do you think the author used questions? *It shows what the character is thinking; it draws the reader into the story*
- How is the boy feeling and how do you know? *Worried and upset – he is thinking of the bad things that might have happened; he is calling Barry's name and crying*
- Does the boy speak on this page? *Only to shout, "Barry! Barry!"*
- Why did the author use speech and exclamation marks here? *To emphasise and shock – the shout breaks out suddenly from his thoughts to shock the reader*

Turn back to **Respond and return** on page 7

Name: _____ **Date:** _____

Reread pages 13–15 of the story and answer the following questions.

Where is the boy?
_____
_____
_____

What can he see?
_____
_____
_____

What can he hear?
_____
_____
_____

How does he feel? Use evidence from the text.
_____
_____
_____

© Pearson Education Ltd, 2008

Bikes, Bombs and Baths: Air Raid!
Skill: Describing settings

Name: _____ **Date:** _____

Make a story plan for 'The Best Skateboard in the World'.
Write notes in the boxes.

Introduction:

Build-up:

Build-up:

Climax:

Resolution (ending):

Bikes, Bombs and Baths: Air Raid!
Skill: Story planning

WRITING PCM 2

Please Write Back

Genre: Wartime fiction
Suggested Renewed Framework Unit: Stories with historical settings
Author: Chris Buckton
Illustrator: Zara Merrick

Key Teaching Objectives

Session 1 / 2
Y4 Strand 1: 1 Justify views; consider alternative opinions
Y4 Strand 7: 2 Deduce characters' reasons for actions / explain how ideas are developed

Session 3 / 4
Y4 Strand 7: 4 Develop understanding of word meanings
Y4 Strand 7: 5 Explain how writers create images / atmosphere
Writing
Y4 Strand 9: 2 Engage readers' interest through setting / characterisation

At a Glance

Session 1 / 2: Focus on Characters
Session 3 / 4: Focus on Setting

This story, told through letters between nine-year-old Maggie and her mum, is an account of being an evacuee in World War II.

The story includes detailed description of setting. Maggie writes about the farm and its country environment. From her mother's letters, the reader also learns about wartime life in a city.

The reader can explore how chronology in the narrative is conveyed by clues in the letters that show time passing.

Maggie's character is clearly communicated through her expressive and descriptive letters. She shares her loves and hates with passion. The children can hunt for clues which show that Maggie is adjusting to life in the country.

Session 1 / 2

Text introduction: activating prior knowledge — Page 22

Ensure that the children know about and understand the evacuation of children to the country during World War II. Use the illustration on page 22 to prompt discussion. Ask them to imagine that they have to get on a train, and go and stay with a family they do not know in a place that is very different from home. Discuss how they might feel. Explain that this story is written in the form of letters.

Teaching strategies

Remind the children to use reading strategies to help them to read new words. Demonstrate as follows:
Write this sentence on the board: 'PPS Please send me a battery for my torch', and cover the word 'battery'. As a group, work out what the covered word says. Uncover the word slowly to check that the children's guesses sound right (phonic), look right (graphic), fit that part of the sentence (grammatical) and make sense (context). Reread the sentence each time to check.

Read and discuss: interpretive strategies — Pages 22–33

Ask the children to read independently to the end of page 27 and to think about what kind of person Maggie is. Discuss the story as a group:

- What have we learnt about the Browns' house? *Farm in the country, outside toilet, animals, muddy*
- How is Maggie feeling? How do you know? *Homesick; always wants her mum to write back*
- Look at the end of Maggie's second letter. Are there any signs that she is getting used to her new home? *She gave her vest to the kittens, she enjoyed the roast chicken*
- How can you tell that there is a change in time between the letters being sent? *She got the vest from her mum, feelings starting to change as time passes*

Tell the children to read the rest of the story and to look out for signs that Maggie is beginning to like her new home:

- 'I wonder why Maggie tells her mum not to bother with the blouse.' *She is wearing David's overalls; perhaps she is enjoying wearing country clothes*
- How is Maggie feeling on page 32? How do you know? *Very happy; doesn't ask her mum to write back*
- Why does Mum say they may be able to come and fetch Maggie? *No bombing*
- Does Maggie go home? How do we know? *Yes; she writes a thank-you letter from home*

▶ Focus on: Characters • Pages 26–27

Respond and return: deduction — Pages 31–33

- How does Maggie feel about the Browns at the end of the story?
- Which phrases in Mum's letter tell you that she will be happy to have Maggie home? *'Please write back'; 'we all miss you'*

Follow-up
PCM 3 Identifying characters

Session 3 / 4

Text introduction: monitoring understanding
Pages 22–33

Discuss how this story is different to other stories. *It is told through an exchange of letters*
Explain that we learn about two different settings in this story: the city, where Mum and Dad are, and the farm in the country, where Maggie is. Ask the children to remember descriptions of the farm and city and to record them in a grid on a piece of paper.

Teaching strategies
Remind the children that verbs often have a suffix added: 's', 'ed', 'ing'. It is important that they check the end of words carefully, so that their reading sounds right. Demonstrate with the sentence: 'I'm staying (stay, stays, stayed) on a farm.'
Remind the children that stories are often written in the past tense, so they contain verbs with the 'ed' ending (morpheme). The letters in this story also describe things happening in the present, e.g. 'Mr Brown kills the hens'; 'Fancy you growing lettuce'.
Write the sentences: 'The cat had kittens. They just pop/pops/popped out.' Ask the children to decide which verb ending sounds right in the sentence and to justify their choice.

Read and discuss: interpretive strategies
Pages 22–33

Tell the children to reread the story independently and to find other descriptions of life in the city and on the farm. During independent reading, observe each child reading and:
1. Prompt and praise the use of reading strategies: *I like the way you checked the end of that word. Look carefully at the end of that verb; it has a suffix that makes it a past tense verb. Read the sentence again and check that it sounds right.*
2. Ask them questions about the setting:
- What do you learn about the farm in the letter on pages 22–23? *In the country; outside toilet*
- What do you learn about the air raids in the city on page 24? *Really bad; fifteen planes; lots of fires*
- Maggie tells us a lot about the farm in her letter on pages 26–27. Can you tell me one of the things she describes? *Carthorse – huge*

 Focus on: Setting • Pages 28–29

Respond and return: interpretive strategies
Pages 22–33

Return to the grid that lists descriptions of the farm and city. Split the group in two. Ask the children to search for descriptions of either the farm or the city to add to the grid. Discuss differences between the city and the country:
- What are the biggest differences?
- 'I wonder why it would be difficult for Maggie to adjust to living in the country.'

Follow-up
PCM 4 Describing settings in a letter

Synopsis
Maggie has been evacuated from the city to live with the Browns on a farm in the country. She writes letters to her mum to tell her about her new experiences.

Initially Maggie hates everything about her new home: the food, the house, the farm, the lack of shops and especially the nine-year-old boy, David. Her mother writes back to comfort her but gives bad news of the air raids.

By the third letter, we can infer that Maggie is beginning to like her new life and has taken to gardening. In Maggie's short fourth letter, she declares her love for farm life and says she wants to stay for ever.

The final letter is written from her city home, thanking Mr and Mrs Brown and David.

Success criteria
- I can use evidence from the text to describe characters.
- I can use reading strategies to recognise verb tenses.
- I can talk about how setting is built up in a story.

Assessment focus
AF1 Use a range of strategies, including accurate decoding of text, to read for meaning.

AF3 Deduce, infer or interpret information, events or ideas from texts.

Further writing
Pretend you are David and respond to Maggie's thank-you letter. Tell her:
- How you all are now Maggie has gone
- What you have been doing on the farm

Focus on: Characters • Pages 26–27   (Session 1 / 2)

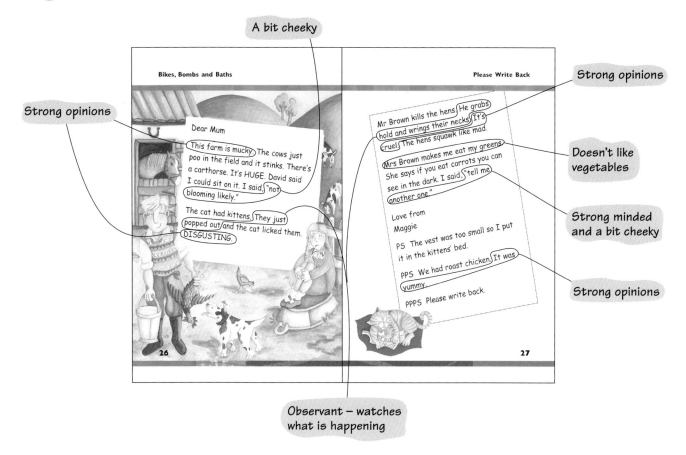

Explain that if we look carefully at this letter, we can learn a lot about Maggie's character.
- Do you think Maggie is interested in the farm? What makes you think this?
- Can you find two examples of Maggie being a little bit cheeky to the Browns?

Maggie seems to either love or hate things. Ask the children to find evidence of her strong opinions.

Look at the line 'This farm is mucky' – how does Maggie feel about the farm? Tell the children to find two other examples of things Maggie doesn't like and one example of something she likes. List the adjectives Maggie uses to describe things: *mucky, disgusting, cruel, yummy*

Discuss what sort of person Maggie is:
'I think Maggie is … because … '

Turn back to **Respond and return** on page 12

Focus on: Setting • Pages 28–29   (Session 3 / 4)

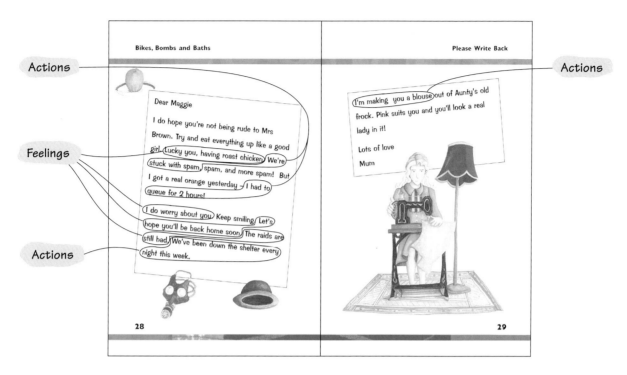

- What setting is described in this letter? *Life in the city during the air raids*
- What do we already know about the city from Mum's first letter? *Bombing is bad, lots of fires, not safe, having to make-do (using an old vest to make a new one for Maggie)*
- Mum writes, 'Lucky you, having roast chicken.' What does this tell you about life in the city? *They can't get much food; life is hard*
- Mum also says, 'I do worry about you' and 'Let's hope you'll be back home soon.' How do you think she is feeling and why? *She is worried that Maggie may be unhappy; she misses Maggie*

Remind the children that authors build up settings by describing actions, feelings, what characters see and what they hear. Ask the children to search the letter for descriptions of actions and record these on a grid as shown below. Tell them to find descriptions of how Mum is feeling. Add these to the grid.

Explain that the author doesn't add descriptions of what Mum sees and hears in this letter. Together, think of one example of what Mum might have seen and heard when she was queuing for the oranges (e.g. lots of people pushing and shoving to get to the front) and during the air raids (e.g. people running for the shelter, searchlights, air raid sirens).
Add these to the grid and discuss how they would add to the description of the setting.

Actions	Feelings	What is seen	What is heard
Eating spam	Lucky having roast chicken	People pushing and shoving to get to the front of the queue	Air raid sirens
Queuing for 2 hours for an orange	Worried		Worried voices
Down the shelter every night	Hopes Maggie will come home soon	People running for the shelter	
Made a blouse out of an old frock	Raids are bad	Searchlights	

Turn back to **Respond and return** on page 13

Name: _____ Date: _____

Part 1

Who said what? Join each quote to the person who said it.

- I do hope you're not being rude to Mrs Brown.
- I hate the food. We had rice pudding.
- I want to come home. I miss you.
- The vest was too small so I put it in the kittens' bed.
- I do worry about you. Keep smiling.
- Here is a plan of my garden.
- I want to stay here FOR EVER.
- We miss you and all your noise!
- Maybe we'll be able to come and fetch you home.

Part 2

Now number Maggie's quotes to show the order she said them in the story.

Bikes, Bombs and Baths: **Please Write Back**

Skill: Identifying characters

Name: _____ Date: _____

Pretend that you are an evacuee and have been sent to a farm in the country.

Write a letter home.

21st April 1941

Dear _____

Describe how you feel: _____
_____
_____

Describe the house: _____
_____
_____

Describe the family: _____
_____
_____

Describe your first meal: _____
_____
_____

Love from _____

PS _____

 Think about

These words might help you:
lonely   miss you   large   cold   smelly   horrible
wanted a boy/girl   greens   carrots   rice pudding   sad

Bikes, Bombs and Baths: Please Write Back
Skill: Describing settings in a letter

WRITING PCM 4

An Octopus in the Bath

Genre: Comical playscript
Suggested Renewed Framework Unit: Stories with historical settings; Plays
Author: Ann Jungman
Illustrator: Andy Hammond

Key Teaching Objectives

Session 1 / 2
Y4 Strand 1: 1 Justify views; consider alternative opinions
Y4 Strand 6: 1 Use phonological / morphological / etymological knowledge to spell new words

Session 3 / 4
Y4 Strand 1: 3 Tell stories effectively / convey information coherently
Y4 Strand 7: 2 Deduce characters' reasons for actions / explain how ideas are developed
Writing
Y4 Strand 9: 2 Engage readers' interest through setting / characterisation

At a Glance

Session 1 / 2: Focus on the Difference between Playscripts and Stories
Session 3 / 4: Focus on Mapping the Build-up of a Scene

This play is set in Roman times and takes place in the north of England. It lends itself to cross-curricular work on this theme.

The story is a comic adventure. The characters' names play on words. The children should relate to the brother and sister, who defy their parents and then save the day.

The family are intended to be upper class and this is reflected in the formal way they speak. The children may need to be introduced to some of the concepts discussed in the play, such as mosaics, bathhouses, Barbarians and Roman history.

Session 1 / 2

Text introduction: activating prior knowledge
Pages 36–41

Ask the children to read the notes on setting (page 36). Ensure that they understand the historical context. Explain that they are going to read a play about a Roman family, where the children defy their parents' wishes and something surprising happens. Write on the board: '"Sir, I've nearly finished the bath," said Grattus.' Talk about how this would be written in a playscript. Look at pages 38–41 and identify the other features of playscripts: *list of characters; scenes instead of chapters; no speech marks or speech verbs; speaker indicated in the margin; stage directions in italic*

Teaching strategies

Write the characters' names on cards. Place them face down on the table. Explain that some of the characters' names may be difficult to read. Ask each child to turn over one card and read the name of their character, decoding it by breaking it down into sounds. They should then show the card to the other children to check the decoding of the name.

Read and discuss: interpretive strategies
Pages 40–55

Explain to the children that they will read Scenes 1 and 2 of the play in this session. Introduce the words 'mosaic' and 'bathhouse'. Remind them to be ready to come in promptly to speak their part. Pause after Scene 1 and ask individuals about 'their' character:
- Grattus: Why do you decide to make a dolphin out of mosaic in the bottom of the bath?
- Horatio: Why do you get annoyed with Muckus and Peculia?
- Diana: Why are you excited about the bathhouse?
- Muckus and Peculia: Why don't you want a dolphin in the bath?

Move on to Scene 2. Read the narrator's lines together. Introduce the words and phrases 'tentacles', 'stuffed dormice' and 'larks' tongues'. Ask the children to read Scene 2 in pairs (one as Muckus and one as Peculia). They should both read the narrator's words silently. Check that the children have understood the plot:
- What do Muckus and Peculia make out of the mosaic? *An octopus*
- How does the octopus look when it is finished? *Scary and ugly; it looks real and creepy when the candles flicker*
- What do Muckus and Peculia hear? *Barbarians on the roof*
- What is their plan? *Muckus creeps out and sounds the alarm; Peculia stays in the bathhouse and sings loudly*

▶ Focus on: the Difference between Playscripts and Stories • Pages 52–53

Respond and return: questioning
Pages 40–55

Hot Seating: Ask one member of the group to be Muckus and another to be Peculia. Invite the other children to ask them questions to find out how they are feeling and what they think will happen next.

Follow-up
PCM 5 Changing text into a playscript

Session 3 / 4

Text introduction: activating prior knowledge
Pages 40–55

Recap what has happened in Scenes 1 and 2. Discuss what is important when performing a play: *making the characters come to life; reading the lines so they sound like the character is talking; actions; body language; props*

Tell the children to turn to page 52. Ask Peculia to say her first line in two ways: first loudly and angrily, then in an anxious whisper. Discuss which is better and why.

Teaching strategies

Remind the children to use reading strategies to help them read new words. Demonstrate as follows:
Write this sentence on the board: 'Five minutes later the lights go on in the house and a gong booms loudly.' Cover the word 'booms'. As a group, work out what the covered word is. Uncover the word slowly to check that the children's guesses sound right, make sense and look right. Reread the sentence or part of the sentence each time to check that it makes sense.

Read and discuss: deduction
Pages 56–63

Introduce the character of Helfur. Remind the children of their parts. Introduce the words and phrases 'dagger', 'warrior', 'villain', 'draw his sword', 'tribe'.
Read Scene 3 as a group. Check that the children have understood the plot:
- Why doesn't Helfur kill Peculia? *Because he sees the octopus, thinks it is real and becomes terrified*
- What does Peculia do that is clever? *She tells Helfur that the octopus is an evil sea creature that attacks people who harm Roman girls*
- Why doesn't Horatio kill the Barbarian? *Because the Barbarian promises to tell his tribe not to attack their house*

Remind the children about tone of voice, pausing and pace. Reread pages 60 and 61 together, focusing on the delivery of the lines.

Focus on: Mapping the Build-up of a Scene
• Pages 56–63

Respond and return: interpretive strategies
Pages 58–62

Read aloud the following lines as indicated. Ask the children to say if they think you have read the lines appropriately and to explain why.

Peculia: *(laughing)* Oh, please don't hurt me. My father will be here in a minute. If you harm me you'll be in trouble.
Horatio: *(whisper slowly)* Drop your dagger, villain, and let my daughter come to me.
Helfur: *(Fearfully)* You have my word as a warrior. We will go back to our side of the wall.

Follow-up
PCM 6 Writing a playscript

Synopsis

The story takes place in a Roman villa near Hadrian's Wall. The mother (Diana) and father (Horatio, the Roman general) decide they would like a mosaic dolphin in their new bathhouse. The children (Muckus and Peculia) complain that this idea is boring.

After dark, the children sneak into the bathhouse and begin to draw and make a mosaic octopus with 16 tentacles. While they are working, they hear a noise on the roof: it is a Barbarian breaking in.

Muckus runs to wake their parents. Helfur, the Barbarian, is about to kill Peculia, when he sees the huge octopus. The rest of the family arrives and the Barbarian promises he will tell his people to leave them alone if they spare him from the monster.

Success criteria

- I can use strategies to read new words.
- I can talk about how characters in a play would speak and behave.
- I can deduce reasons for characters' actions.

Assessment focus

AF1 Use a range of strategies, including accurate decoding of text, to read for meaning.

AF2 Understand, describe, select or retrieve information, events or ideas from texts and use quotation and reference to the texts.

Further writing

Continue the play and write Scene 4.
- How do Muckus and Peculia explain how the octopus ended up on the bottom of the bath?
- What happens at the end?

Focus on: the Difference between Playscripts and Stories • Pages 52–53   (Session 1 / 2)

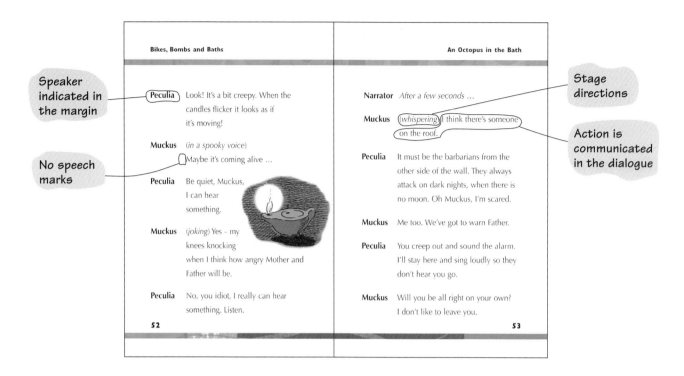

Remind the children that a playscript is written in a different way from a story. Ask them to work in pairs and to see how many differences they can spot.

Prompts:
- What headings can you see?
- How do you know who is speaking?
- How do you know what is happening?
- Why are there no speech marks?

List the children's ideas. Explain that it may be harder to follow the action in a play because it is communicated by the narrator or in the dialogue.

Read Peculia's first line in an anxious whisper. Discuss how Peculia is feeling and how we know. Stress that, in a play, it is what a character says and how they say it that tells us about them. What does this line tell us about Peculia? *She is scared*

Discuss how Muckus responds to Peculia. *Joking*. Practise reading his first line. How would this response make Peculia feel? *Belittled, silly*

- Is Muckus joking or not when he says, "I think there's someone on the roof"? How do you know? *Not joking; stage directions* Ask a member of the group to say his line.

Discuss with the group how Peculia might say "Oh Muckus, I'm scared."

◀ Turn back to **Respond and return** on page 18

Focus on: Mapping the Build-up of a Scene • Pages 56–63   (Session 3 / 4)

Main events in Scene 3:
1. Muckus awakens the house
2. Helfur arrives and threatens Peculia
3. Helfur raises his dagger to kill Peculia
4. Helfur sees the octopus and Peculia tells him it is evil
5. Muckus arrives with their parents
6. Horatio threatens the Barbarian
7. Barbarian promises never to come back
8. The family is safely reunited

Mapping the build-up in Scene 3
Draw a bar graph on the board. As a group, retell the main events in this scene, focusing on the way tension is built up throughout the scene.

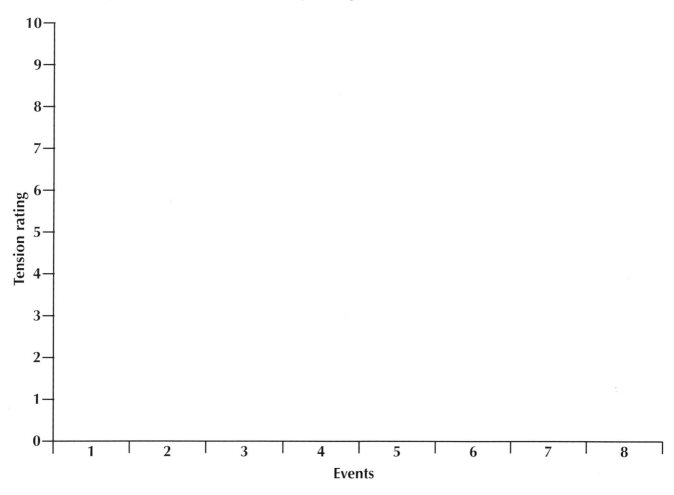

Remind the children about the terms 'climax' and 'resolution' and the fact that the tension in the story builds towards the climax.

Discuss each event in the story and decide on a 'tension' rating (**1** = little tension, **10** = very tense)

Fill in the bar graph and look at how the tension builds and then decreases as the play reaches the resolution.

Turn back to **Respond and return** on page 19

Name: _____   Date: _____

This is what happened after the end of Scene 1.

Change the text below into playscript.

> Muckus and Peculia went to their bedroom. Peculia was angry.
> "Dolphins are stupid!" she said. "Let's make our own mosaic."
> "We can't do that," said Muckus.
> "Yes, we can!" shouted Peculia. "We can do it tonight, when everyone is asleep."
> She jumped up and down in excitement. But Muckus was scared. "It's too dangerous," he whispered.

Narrator

Peculia

Muckus

Peculia

Narrator

Muckus

Bombs, Bikes and Baths: **An Octopus in the Bath**
Skill: Changing text into a playscript

Name: _____ **Date:** _____

Write a scene for another play with the same characters.

Title: **Muckus and Peculia strike again!**

Narrator *Muckus and Peculia become very curious about what is over the wall, so they decide to climb up to take a closer look.*

Peculia

Muckus

Peculia

Narrator *Suddenly Muckus slips and falls over the wall.*

Muckus

Peculia

Muckus

Helfur

Bikes, Bombs and Baths: An Octopus in the Bath
Skill: Writing a playscript

PCM 6

Navigator Max

Written by: Louise Dempsey
Denise Margetts

Teaching Guides advisors: Shirley Bickler
Michael Lockwood

Rigby
Halley Court, Jordan Hill, Oxford, OX2 8SJ

Rigby is an imprint of Pearson Education Limited, a company incorporated in England and Wales, having its registered office at Edinburgh Gate, Harlow, Essex, CM20 2JE. Registered company number: 872828

www.rigbyed.co.uk

Rigby is a registered trademark of Reed Elsevier, Inc, licensed to Pearson Education Limited

© Pearson Education Limited 2008

Firs published 2004

This edition first published 2008

12 11 10 09 08
10 9 8 7 6 5 4 3 2 1

British Library Cataloguing in Publication Data is available from the British Library on request.

ISBN 978 0 433 07873 9

All rights reserved. The material in this publication is copyright. Pupil sheets may be freely photocopied for classroom use in the purchasing institution. However, this material is copyright and under no circumstances may copies be offered for sale. If you wish to use the material in any way other than that specified you must apply in writing to the publishers.

Typeset by Red Giraffe
Illustrated by Max Ellis (cover); Lisa Smith (page 5); Serina Curmi (pages 8–9); Zara Merrick (pages 14–16); Andy Hammond (page 20)
Logo artwork by Max Ellis
Printed in the UK by Ashford Colour Press

Every effort has been made to contact copyright holders of material reproduced in this book. Any omissions will be rectified in subsequent printings if notice is given to the publishers.